THE
APARTMENT
OF
TRAGIC
APPLIANCES

THE
APARTMENT
OF
TRAGIC
APPLIANCES

MICHAEL D. SNEDIKER

THE APARTMENT OF TRAGIC APPLIANCES
© MICHAEL D. SNEDIKER, 2013

First published in 2013 by
Peanut Books
a literary offshoot of
punctum books
Brooklyn, NY
http://punctumbooks.com

ISBN-13: 978-0615792484
ISBN-10: 0615792480

Library of Congress Cataloging Data is available
from the Library of Congress.

ACKNOWLEDGMENTS

"Concerto Grosso," *notnostrums*, issue 5

"Ganymede," "The Apartment of Tragic
   Appliances," *Blip Magazine*, Winter 2011

"Elegy for Marni," "Jane Eyre," "Some Big News,"
   Maggy, February 2012

"It's Volleyball, Not Sexism," "Specimen Day,"
   Fatboy Review, Summer 2011

"Rabbit," *jubilat* 20

When the bottom of the sea
is falling in,
    we hang in space
our fingers clinging to the minutes
    of our last meeting.

    --Fanny Howe
      "The Confessions of Persephone"

When I consider how our houses are built
and paid for, or not paid for, and their internal
economy managed and sustained, I wonder that
the floor does not give way under the visitor while
he is admiring the gewgaws upon the mantel-piece...

    --Henry David Thoreau, *Walden*

Appliqué

In this version of the myth, Orpheus moves
Persephone to tears because at this point nearly
anything will move her to tears, and because
she can't bear that this poet has traveled to the
Underworld for the sake of Eurydice and not
her—Persephone needs an exit plan, too.

Why do I remember the Persephone myth as an
ancient Cymbalta commercial? Winter is when
mommy's sad? Who teaches this sort of thing?
That Demeter is a depressive is one thing; that
Persephone is stuck in the Underworld is another.
Persephone has enough on her plate (namely,
seeds) without worrying about the crops of some
other country. She can't be held responsible for
everything.

In this version, Persephone is a gay man in
provincial Ontario. She misses Massachusetts.
(Her mother is lovely.) She is no longer with
Hades, who was beautiful but cold; she forgave
him his limitations a while back. No longer with
Hades, but still in the Underworld: for the time
being, that's how it is.

If Orpheus isn't going to save her, she'll write
her own poems. They won't spring her from the
Underworld, but they remind her that if days
and nights can be salvaged, so perhaps can she.
We find Persephone in the *mise en abyme* of a girl
reading a myth about a girl writing a myth.

In this *trauerspiel*, the villain is a landlady who
lets Persephone's rented apartment fall to pieces.
Trapped in the typology of myth, Persephone is all
the more rattled when nothing works.

Appliances are supposed to make the world a
little easier. This apartment of broken things has
something else to teach her. As Wittgenstein
writes at the opening of the *Tractatus*, it will
"perhaps only be understood by those who have

themselves already thought the thoughts which are expressed in it—or similar thoughts."

Or as Walter Benjamin writes, "That which lies here in ruins, the highly significant fragment, the remnant, is, in fact, the finest material in baroque creation. For it is common practice in the literature of the baroque to pile up fragments ceaselessly without any strict idea of a goal, and in the unremitting expectation of a miracle, to take the repetition of stereotypes for a process of intensification."

We have here a pile-up. In taking repetition for intensification, we have a mistaking. It's said that we wouldn't recognize Greek temples if they weren't ruins. This is how Persephone feels about her apartment. Benjamin suggests that "allegories are, in the realm of thoughts, what ruins are in the realm of things." In this sense, Persephone lives in an allegory and thinks ruinously.

Unremitting: somewhere there's a potsherd depicting the Eleusinian mystery as Lucille Ball scarfing chocolates from an assembly line.

Imagine the still without Ethel, without the supervisor, without the chocolates. Roland Barthes meets Lucy meets Persephone: every ruin tells the story of its own sanctifying.

TABLE OF CONTENTS

CONCERTO GROSSO

I leave a radio on like a light for my return from
campus. Gay sadness—the leashes it takes and
gives. The radio is on for it, to keep it occupied
in my absence. When I return from teaching,
the radio is playing one of my favorites, the
Mendellssohn concerto where Felix is throwing
plates at Cécile Jeanrenaud, and then at the
surprising tail end of a *Tempo semplice*, he
accuses her in English of never truly having
communicated the extent of her loyalty. She
insists in broken German she thought her loyalty
a given. At which point all her languages break.
She riffles through them for one that seems fluent,
but duress has made fluency itself the missing
thing. *If only I were articulate* slipping into *if only
I were fluent, graceful,* or does this mean *if only he
were graceful.* Sometimes I leave the radio on as a
nostalgic fiction, the sort of thing that might have
assuaged someone decades previous, like this
might trick the gay sadness into considering its
own *Antique Roadshow* quaintness, provenance
and value apprised only after the fact, which
might be the first step in learning to take it less
seriously. *And what can you tell us about this sadness,
do you have any idea how old it is, or what it's worth?*
Cue *schadenfreude* for the duped: *ecce* radio. But
how to fine-tune nostalgic and sad—poor Cécile,
the world so unkind, what can she say to counter
her husband's sense that things get more brittle
as each attempt at lubrication or leavening on
either side leaves them both, it seems, further
dilapidated. The loneliness was *allegro* then *largo*
then *subito*. And as I turn the key another plate
remembers crashes.

GANYMEDE

When one decides past certain hours to go to
SUBWAY (*eatfresh*) despite a decent earlier
serving of asparagus vichyssoise, one thinks,
I'll feel a little less abject about the excursion
if I travel with a nice accessory, for instance an
envelope-sized Louis Vuitton satchel on whose
veracity one has insisted on past occasions,
although not this particular night. Less junket
than one is junk, raccooning down the sidewalk
to where one's students might be gorging,
shoulder-slung with an object Hawthorne might
describe as a citizen of somewhere else. Oh Louis,
strung between the Actual and the Imaginary,
like something in moonlight, cobwebbed or
embroidered with the enthusiasm of an allegorical
crazy person shriving for someone else's bungle.
And so one embarks, +more or less sober, maybe
further sobered by the unfolding event, or as
likely, sobriety floundering in the Hawthornian
threshold as though this kabuki gravitas could
help the other more glaringly deflating elements
of a binge-before-sleep pass unnoticed. As though
the seriousness emanating from the bag might
not, in fact, lead to further pathos, one's seeming
by others, employees and otherwise, slightly
deranged: Aschenbach bringing a little *LV* bag
down to the Lido. When one arrives at SUBWAY
(*eatfresh*), one hopes for neither recognition nor
blandishment beyond the sandwich. One is
unprepared, entering such an establishment past
midnight with the shredding dignity of a heroine
at the end of a Wharton novel, for comments
about the bag, comments that seem to interpellate
the bag as a romantic shibboleth. This isn't the
idea. Dear reader, I brought the bag for dignity,
underestimating the extent to which such a bag
might flag me as more than an appetite on the
other side of a hygienic counter. And so: when
one of the workers says to one upon arriving at the
front of the hygienic sandwich-making counter,

I really like your bag, one is a little thrown off, as
one was wishing to seem formidable, not needing
to be there, as though meeting a lesser relative
at an unfortunate train station, who me, no you
must have me confused with one who comes
here often. I'm waiting for someone. If one had
made the mistake of wearing a large puce hat with
plumes, one would readjust the hat, reminding
him of the larger Darwinian scaffolding from
which one only temporarily had dropped. One
would say something minute in acknowledgment
of the appreciation, even as one couldn't know
the degree to which one's reply missed or matched
the flavor of his comments. In the splendid ides
of humanism, Cavafy might say yes, it's a nice
bag; or, yes we have found each other like shelter
animals on opposite sides of a hygienic counter,
and this is just the beginning of an unavoidable
Proustian dance only superficially for the sake
of a sandwich. Or, yes, it is a nice bag—and how
bolstering in the epiphany of one's humiliation
to be interested in this boy's unexpected spume
of interest, as though interest were the accessory
with which, from the outset, one might have
traveled, even as proleptic interest in the moment
seemed not only implausible but its own problem.
To walk into a SUBWAY (*eatfresh*) at so late an
hour anticipating that something of interest
would occur, because the excursion might be
interesting, hence bringing along the bag—no,
this was unreasonable. We were naked in his
fawning, which added to the prescient sense of
disgrace (insofar as one can anticipate disgrace
more easily than one can track interest), in the
way one seasoning disrupts seasonings from a
different region. One is a vichyssoise in need of a
little tarragon, and despite his Anglo-Saxon milky
countenance, his observation about the bag is a
festive sneeze of paprika. One debates whether
one spoons it out fast, or stirs it in, or just watches

it like swamp guck settling on the surface before
sinking. Maybe even inadvertently signaling more
paprika, as though this was what the soup had
always wanted. At which point the employee
asks *what one wants*, as though this under such
circumstances were an unloaded question. My life
had stood a loaded gun, but never had Dickinson
waded through such a congerie of irrelevant
feelings. She wouldn't have brought the bag,
rowing in Eden, deliberating turkey over meatball.
Does one say *turkey* to be the stronger one, with
an ear for the decorous or didactic, Saint Francis
and his lewd bird across the hygienic counter,
sent by the Lord for this lesson alone? Neither was
learning. His hands, in gloves the size of plastic
bags, were a reminder that the situation called for
prophylactics. And then the further harassment
of *what would you like on that*. At this point (to
keep from weeping), one says lettuce. One orders
something, oh heartbreak for everything, without
recalling what it is. One wants this over with. And
like a boulder dropped from his pelvis into one's
own, or near it, the employee says *you know I have
the wallet*. One doesn't know what to say, and like
Dickinson on the verge of death one's metaphors
crash and burn; as critics suggest, sometimes
her metaphors just break off when they least
understand themselves. Whatever she says at this
point is up to whoever finds me holding you in
hand, satchel over shoulder, Aeneas raccooning
through the dungeon gates.

MANHUNT

I'd never seen so many jockstraps in my life.
There were side shots of men in which the
elastic around their asses made them look more
like Pac-Man than they did already. The elastic
straps turned asses into arcade heroes hungry
for pac-dots, trying to avoid Blinky, Pinky, Inky,
and Clyde, otherwise known as Shadow, Speedy,
Bashful, and Pokey. An arcade hero in search of
fruits: maybe this was subliminal. Maybe I was
reading into it. Nine times out of ten it turned
out the members with jockstrap profile shots
were self-described bottoms, which made either
the jockstrap or the stated sexual preference
gratuitous. There was a lot of gratuitous going
on, and *saudade*. If other members were thinking
about side-profile jockstrap shots in terms of
Pac-Man, they probably weren't thinking about
avoiding Pokey. Maybe it was just me. There was
a profile pic taken by a member standing with his
camera pointed at his erection. All one could see
in the pic was part of a T-shirt, the erection, and
two feet. There were a lot of headless horsemen.
It was like Washington Irving with nudity; it was
Washington Irving without Christina Ricci. What
made this picture different from countless others
taken from the same angle was that this member
had inverted the colors such that his erection
appeared in the photograph an icy blue. It looked
like an ice sculpture for a bris, surrounded by
cantaloupe teeth and cocktail shrimp. Maybe it
was melting. It reminded me of Laura Palmer's
head unfurled from its body bag. *I want hot action*,
it said, and simultaneously, *I'm numb, I'm blue*. I
had to look things up; there were a lot of acronyms
in which members were either very interested or
from which they recoiled. Some of the frontal
jockstrap pics (as opposed to the side shots) made

it look like crotches were wearing preventative
surgical masks. A lot of them looked like close-ups
of hypochondriacs or dental hygienists. There
were profile pics that looked too good to be true.
CrazyFunGuy reclined on satin like a Barberini
faun. Maybe he'd gone to a Sears Portrait Studio,
maybe he chose satin the way parents choose
beach buckets. I needed other options. I was
looking for someone whose loneliness matched
the contours of my own. This wasn't an option.

CANADA DAY (I)

In honor of Canada Day, I left my apartment.
There were a lot of middle-aged women posing
by the steam engine. There were a lot of people
wearing T-shirts that said CANUCK or implied
CANUCK with maple leaves. In honor of Canada
Day, the Prince George was a cash bar with paper
cups. After drinks at the Prince George, we
walked to the Royal Duke for more drinks. All
the pubs were named after British royalty, even
as Canada Day was meant to celebrate Canada's
no longer being British. On Canada Day, Duke
seemed a better name for a Basset Hound. After
the Royal Duke, we went to someone's loft for a
surprise party for the partner of the director of
the town's queer film festival. I'd never been to
the film festival. I could imagine its qualities. The
festival director and his partner were en route. We
and the other guests hid in the bedrooms. I was in
a bedroom with nobody I knew. This turned out
to be untrue, insofar as it turns out I'd IM'd half
of the men in the bedroom on Manhunt. When
the director and his partner got home, we flung
ourselves from the bedrooms like bats, screaming
surprise.

ELEGY FOR MARNI

Let's ricochet. Let's have him followed. He walks
real fast. He's walked right out of a Giacomo
Balla. His legs are futurist paint. Let's give him a
paper parasol and see if he can open it without
breaking. Trying to open a parasol for the first
time is scarier than he imagines. Standing under
a paper parasol makes him feel like a fun cocktail.
He feels garnished. Or maybe he's thinking along
the lines of the "tropical flakes" which a certain
fish was never given on account of his bad advice.
Marni, little quiverer, bluer than sapphires but
less resilient. He'd said "once a week" but should
have said, as the "tropical flakes" container states,
"two to three times daily." Leave it to someone
with an eating disorder to force an eating disorder
on a fish. Let's all for a moment pause and think
of Marni, who led a vibrant but really short life.
In order to open the paper parasol, completely
open it, he needed to work it back and forth like
something he hadn't anticipated as sexual. It felt
like he was trying not to hurt the parasol. He
treated it like a person. For the sake of instruction,
they looked at an etching in the living room of
three schoolgirls holding paper parasols. Two
of the girls were smiling, one of them more
nervously than the other. The third girl seemed
not to like being etched or looked at. To which
we responded, "We're not looking at you, we're
looking at your parasol to figure out how to open
his. We're trying to learn something here." Our
parasol appeared identical to hers in terms of
trestles, something between a Noguchi and a
McQueen. Upon closer inspection, it seemed the
discomfited girl was propping up her parasol with
her hand, keeping it open rather than holding
it by its handle. Maybe that's what her face was
about, her *moue*. Let's pose him with his parasol

beneath the etching. Let's brainstorm. Let's swap ideas without realizing they're nearly the same, the reflection of ideas in a pond just after you skip a stone. For instance, that roses open without the effort of parasols. If parasols only needed sun, there would be no reason for this poem. And if roses needed such dexterity this would be a different poem altogether. Imagine having this relationship with a rose. Carefully, each morning, working the sepals. You don't need to get involved. You can mostly watch, which is what we do. The parasol, the glimmering fish: these were different stories. These were fish stories. They happened every day.

CLEMENZO

If it seems like something out of Racine, it
usually is. As in Titus Flavius Vespasianus, Holy
Roman Emperor, over the moon for Berenice
(pronounced like *very spicy*), ruler of Judaea,
daughter of King Herod Agrippa. The Holy
Roman Emperor falling in love with the ruler
of Judaea equals *problemo*. Equals Danny Zuko
falling in love with Sandy Olsen. *Look at me,
look at me*, I'm Sandra, ruler of Judaea, and you
have an empire to shepherd which kiboshes
our idyll before it happens. *Tell me more tell me
more, did you get very far*, no, because he's the
Holy Roman Emperor. *Uh well-a well-a well-a
huh*. Except (this being Racine) that Olivia
Newton-John is Christian (or at least has
recorded Christmas albums) and John Travolta
is a Scientologist (although performs on Olivia
Newton-John's *Christmas Wish*). Maybe the
Emperor of Scientology could have dallied
with Berenice without the Christians and other
non-Scientologists cracking jokes behind her
back, all poodle skirt and milkshake. Australia
as always is a euphemism. Mostly, Titus could
have been with Berenice without the empire
roiling, but this being Racine and eventually
Mozart, the dalliance only further enrages Vitellia,
daughter of Vitellius, usurped emperor, who (i.e.
Vitellia) for the sake of symmetry we'll call Betty
Rizzo, who pines for Danny Zuko, their shared
vowels. Hence Vitellia deciding on account of
Zuko's infatuation with Berenice to have Zuko
assassinated and ditto his flagship Rome burnt to
cinders. But then, whoa, hold the phone, Zuko
calls Sandy off for the sake of his empire. He's
to marry another Scientologist for the sake of
imperial stability, whatever that looks like. I don't
like imagining John Travolta in a toga but there it
is, and there he's picking as his second affianced
a Scientologist other than Betty Rizzo, namely
Servilia. This is big. Betty, enraged even more

than before, calls back aforesaid assassination and arson, earlier called off post-Sandy. Meanwhile, Servilia, a mezzo in trousers, loves someone else (who could blame her), and Zuko, God bless him (or whomever), frees her from conjugal obligation, insofar as her fidelity to her guy (or whatever) reminds him, plangently, of his broken fidelity to Olivia Newton-John, if only his fidelity could have been explored without totally jeopardizing the empire. Cue Racine. Cue Vitellia, again, who isn't pleased that after Berenice there comes Servilia. So the assassination is on, a minion named Sextus pilfering poison, watching for the right moment and chalice. But whoa, *tell me more tell me more,* the marriage with Servilia is off. At this point, we might be thinking that Titus, like other certain Holy Romans, plays for the other team, insofar as he keeps huffing about marriages then piously precluding them, like a Jamesian, which makes him seem more and less Travoltan. But then there's Vitellia, and once the Servilia marriage is off (like not having to suffer through *Grease 2*), she (Vitellia) gets what she always wanted. Harbingers descend upon Vitellia's chaise to announce with all obligatory pomp that Titus, finally, finally, wants to marry her. But the assassination (not to mention arson of Rome) is still on (!!!), and Vitellia is like *oh YAY, I get my man* and in the next operatic breath *OH FUCK, he's about to be killed, at my orders, not to mention Rome (!!!).* So she's wailing front-stage as the harbingers think she's crazy in love, for love, with love. As opposed to her actual *FUCK FUCK FUCK.* What is she to do. Plots thicken, thin, *uh well-a-well-a-well-a-huh.*

CANADA DAY (2)

In honor of Canada Day, I wanted to let him know
I could have my way with him. At the same time,
I barely had a way. He could barely walk up my
three flights of stairs. Before having if not my way
then some clichéd way, I gave him a glass of water
and a bowl of raspberries. His belly button was
the biggest outie I'd ever seen. It was the size of a
berry. This was a distraction. A further distraction
were his teeth, which looked like they were
missing an important genetic sequence, as though
nothing had told the teeth not to sprout from
their gums any which way. The next morning,
his stagger was replaced by a lack of courtesy that
couldn't be chalked up to hangover. He looked
at my body for a long time. I asked what he was
thinking. He said he was thinking about the
varicose veins along my ankles. As he lay on top
of me, scrutinizing my body's flaws, we discussed
whether the given clarinet concerto on the radio
was Mozart. He said it wasn't, and it turns out
he was right, but he also asked naïve questions
about radios, like whether there were radios in
Europe. I still had strands of plastic turquoise
on my body from a wig. He picked the strands
from my body like a gorilla at nits. After a while,
wearing one of my beach hats, he stopped talking.
He just assessed and stood around. I wondered
why he was still there. When he finally turned to
walk down the steps, I asked if he was going to say
goodbye. He asked if I wanted him to say goodbye
and I said no, I didn't want him to say goodbye. In
honor of Canada Day, he didn't.

THE GRAIN & THE GRAPE

This is an important fable. I heard it on the way to
a Shad Bake that was also a fable, the moral of one
being not so different from the other. All fables, in
the end, have some structural and moral overlaps,
e.g. "The Servant Girl Justified" (wherein a wife
asks *Has not your spouse with you a right to try what
freaks he likes*) and "The Eel Pie" (wherein the hero
of sorts, the fable's learner, cries *I'm surfeited, 'tis
far too much: Pie ev'ry day! and nothing else to touch!*).
The titular and thematic similarities between "The
Shad Bake" and "The Eel Pie" go without saying;
maybe redundancy is necessary given the human
condition (i.e. incorrigibly not learning from past
events). By the end of the Shad Bake, who didn't
want some pie, who didn't want something other
than shad? The morals of most fables suggest
that the thing about which one is most excited
isn't what one thought it was or that one should
have been wanting something else (or nothing)
all along. In another fable which we could call
"The Dim Lake That Looked Less Shallow in the
Gloaming," a boy tells his lover that he feels abject
when he (the lover) makes him brush his teeth
and wash his hands after sneaking a cigarette,
but the misunderstanding lover thinks that the
boy doesn't really mean "abject" on account of
his "expansive" vocabulary, to which the boy
responds, my vocabulary isn't just "expansive,"
it's exacting, when I say "abject" I mean it. Along
the lines of Winnicott's observation that the only
thing that could have rescued Hamlet would have
been reading *Hamlet*, the boy needed a copy of
"The Dim Lake That Looked Less Shallow in the
Gloaming." Something analogous could be said of
the Eel Pie and the Shad Bake. All gluttons from
certain vantages are gluttons for punishment,
and ditto the girl in "The Grain & the Grape."
You can buy fifty clothespins for less than two
dollars, but you can't buy insight. The heroine
of our fable is unaware of her lack of insight,

distracted by the Lady of the Lake, otherwise
known as the TSS Earnslaw, a vintage screw
steamer on Lake Wakatipu. It was Queenstown,
and they'd just finished, she and her Dad, a bit
of vineyarding in the heart of Otego. Vineyards
in a fable named Mount Difficulty and Wooing
Tree might have been a tip-off for someone with
insight, but the girl and her dad, increasingly less
lucid and coordinated, had quaffed Difficulty and
Wooing like jugs of Gallo. After Otego, they were
back at the wharf, reading the plaque in front of
Earnslaw, as Earnslaw (a pretty good name for
the Lady of a Lake) gleamed above them like an
ancient lacquered temple. And then, like the
God-Beyond-God which Paul Tillich describes
as *both the courage of despair and the courage in and
above every courage*, the girl and her dad espy, past
Earnslaw, blue neon. It was *minus 5°*, a very cool-
looking ice bar. Like most things in fables, it was
very cool on several registers. After vineyarding,
the girl and her dad think why not. A hostess
shepherds them into an antechamber, gruffs
them into winter jackets and boots, everything
shearling. The requisite shearling makes the
bar seem both cool and preppy, like a country
club requiring fleecy blazers. And so they're
shepherded into the bar, a buzzing igloo, where
everyone looks similarly sheepish. If the girl,
parka hood squashing the grosgrain bow into
her hair, had an eye for irony, she might think
they all were wolves in disguise. She wasn't quite
there. Everything inside was ice. They were
waspy tourist Inuits. The only non-icy things
were the cash register and liquor bottles. These
were ordinary. The girl and her dad ponied into
ice-stools and ordered *42 Below*, which referred
less to the temperature than New Zealand's being
forty-two degrees below the equator. Sometimes
how cold one is describes both how one feels
and where one is. Sometimes one loses track of

space and time altogether because all one feels
is cold, which takes us back to "The Dim Lake
That Looked Less Shallow in the Gloaming," to
the extent that a shallow lake will both melt and
freeze more quickly than deeper water. Which
takes us back to the girl guzzling vodka from an ice
funnel. The vodka was feijoa-flavored, also known
as guavasteen, also known as *Acca sellowiana*,
whose fruit, when immature, is white and opaque
(cf. "The Dim Lake"), and, generally speaking,
somewhat tolerant, which actually means not as
tolerant as one would wish (cf. "The Dim Lake").
But distilled, it goes down easy, especially through
a funnel. After guzzling, she chomped the funnel
down, like all the other customers chewing their
ice cups out of sexual frustration or whatever,
before the ice melted their incorrigibly melting
mouths.

OUIJA

I hunch over cupcakes doing my exercises. One
arm stretches heavenward while I balance on my
toes, strengthening my Achilles' heel and abs.
One might say I was working several muffin tops
at once. It wasn't easy, this simultaneous stretch
& hunch as my non-stretched arm dropped
grapes into the muffin tins. I didn't want a repeat
of the previous weekend's strawberry disaster.
I was a flamingo. I couldn't get the Boredom
Proneness Scale out of my head. Two-thirds of the
population scored between 81 and 117. Only 2.3%
scored above 135 or below 63. I rocked a 138 and
was trying to be humble about the results. A 138
meant I was non-prone to boredom, as indicated
by the enthusiasm with which I contemplated
the Proneness Scale. Meanwhile the cupcakes
were going okay, better than the strawberries.
Out of nowhere, past the sound of fragging and
lawnmowers, came a voice. *KNOCK ONCE IF YOU
CAN HEAR US.* Huh? I shouted, *Jeff, are you back
from Bomster, what's up with the "knock" thing?* No
answer. And then the voice, which may as well
have been rising from muffin batter, *KNOCK ONCE.* I
exchanged glances with myself, got off my tiptoes.
It dawned on me that maybe this kitchen full of
cupcakes was a mini-rapture. I rapped knuckles
on the counter, once, then waited. And the same
voice, nearly recognizable, asked *IF THIS IS MABEL.
KNOCK ONCE IF THIS IS MABEL, KNOCK TWICE IF IT'S
SOMEONE ELSE.* I knocked twice. *THEN WHO IS THIS?*
It was like I was on the other side of a Ouija
board. *KNOCK ONCE IF YOU KNOW MABEL.* I rapped
my knuckles twice. *KNOCK ONCE IF YOU ARE IN THE
SPIRIT WORLD.* You'd think if one were raptured
one would be the first to know. I improvised
without an ort of boredom. I spoke sonorously
into the late-Spring pollen streaming through

the screen door: *I'm making cupcakes.* There was
a pause. I continued. *I have things,* I called, *to say
to Cathy.* I imagined letters on a Ouija board as
the teacup lurched. It seemed Cathy wasn't there.
Meanwhile, the cupcakes had been transferred
from counter to oven, and as I watched them spill
golden, I went vatic in a Southern accent. *AH SAY,
WHUT'S TRAGIC FER YOU IN'T NECESSARILY TRAGIC FER
ME.* No one liked the accent, and just in the nick
of time, as there were too many cupcakes to finish.
Even as I relished telling this story at the next
party over soup shots and stone-fruit sangria, only
sometimes wondering if anyone could see or hear
me. This had been an ongoing question.

JANE EYRE

My usual mood of humiliation fell on embers. I
was in the mood for being useful or officious. It
appeared he was not in the mood to notice us.
His changes of mood did not offend me. He was,
in short, in his after-dinner mood. There was
something off in the paroxysm which seized him
when he expressed his mood. He was moody, too.
I believed his moodiness. In his present fractious
mood, she dared not whisper observations.
That restless, excited mood which hurried into
darkening. I was fully aware that only serious
moods were acceptable. A singular mood came
over me. No new allusion was made to the subject
over which I brooded. I walked slowly to enjoy
the species of my brooding. Besides his frequent
absences, another barrier to friendship was his
brooding. We brooded over bliss. I sought my
bedroom to brood over it. In his countenance
I saw a change that looked brooding. A puerile
tear dimmed my eye. I wiped my tears, fearful
anyone would comfort me. A wretchedness kept
drawing from me silent tears. After drinking
some coffee, I swallowed the remainder with
some tears. Left to myself, my tears watered the
boards. She wiped a tear from her cheek. Tears,
hot and large, had continually been scalding my
cheek. While trying to devour my tears, I was
seized by a fit of coughing. Some natural tears
shed on being told this. A few words would bring
tears to your eyes. He stopped and burst into
tears. My tears had risen as in childhood. Neither
of us had dropped a tear. My tears gushed out.
I was so hurt by her coldness that tears rose to
my eyes. A tear of impatience. Ashamed of it, I
wiped it away. I was preparing for a hot rain of
tears. Besides, the floodgates of tears were open.
I had been struggling with tears for some time. I

had taken pains to repress them, because I knew
he would not like to see me weep. I let them
flow as freely and long as they liked. If the flood
annoyed him, so much the better. I interrupted,
furtively dashing some tears from my eyes. The
tears gushed to her eyes. I was suffocating with the
bitterest tears. The trace of tears was doubtless.
The bitter check had wrung from me some tears.
So much hurt that tears started to my eyes. More
than once, my tears blistered the page. I saw a tear
slide. The last letter I received drew tears. I gushed
and brooded, moodily. I brooded on my moody
gushing. I wiped it away.

COUPLES JEOPARDY

We were on the rocks. Even so, we were reluctant
to throw in the towel; or whenever we threw
it we ended up picking it up again with sighs
of exasperation. I sat with the towel, flipping
channels, landing on *JEOPARDY!* It was satisfying
to blurt questions with confidence. Unlike my
better half, it gave me answers. Sometimes I asked
the right question. "'Up' Songs" for $400. *After
they fell asleep at the drive-in the Everly Brothers had
this to say.* "Wake Up Little Susie," I blurt. I quickly
correct myself, "What is Wake Up Little Susie?"
Sometimes Alex Trebek would make a troubled,
prodding face, like he believed in me. *In the
psychology of learning, it's "the retention of association,"
in "Cats", it's a showstopping song.* "What are
memories," which I quickly revise. "What is
memory?" Just before commercial break, Alex
Trebek announced something unprecedented.
Given the success of *COLLEGE JEOPARDY!* and
CELEBRITY JEOPARDY! they were looking for
contestants for *COUPLES JEOPARDY!* When my
better half got home, I said that I'd been watching
JEOPARDY! while he was out wherever, and Alex
Trebek had announced some casting call for a
special *COUPLES JEOPARDY!* Back in the day, my
better half would have caught the irony, but right
now he was mostly thinking *money.* Neither of
us was thinking this might save our relationship,
even as on some level I thought if *COUPLES
JEOPARDY!* couldn't save our relationship maybe
it could serve as proof that maybe we just weren't
in the cards. We MapQuested the nearest mall
that was holding auditions and went to bed. On
the day of the audition, my better half was better
than expected. One of the *JEOPARDY!* interns
asked for the French name for meat served in its
own juice, and my better half buzzed in before
the rest of the couples, *What is au jus?* We were
meat in our own juice, he knew that. He was
stewing, and knew I was also stewing, but that

he knew it in French. Several hours passed like this. Sometimes it almost felt like love; we did high-fives. When we made it onto *COUPLES JEOPARDY!*, I didn't tell our friends or relatives. I considered our outfits for weeks in advance. Matching versus not matching. Alex Trebek was taller in real life than I'd expected; he looked like Bill Clinton. I could imagine having an affair with Alex Trebek. My better half and I were up against Robin and Larry and Mitchell and Denice. Robin and Larry were both schoolteachers. Alex said, *So, Robin, Larry says you're famous for a very special party trick.* Robin glared at Larry, *I am? What party trick? What did you tell Alex? I thought we filled out the form together.* This was how things went. Denice grabbed the buzzer from Mitchell and snapped each time he tried to reclaim it. My better half and I disagreed about categories. I wanted "Faux Pas" and my better half wanted "The Heavyweight Champ." I shrugged theatrically, as though to communicate to Alex that *this is how it was.* During Final Jeopardy ("Battles"), Robin scratched out Larry's question and replaced it with an intentionally wrong question, not even phrased as a question. "And what did you wager?" Alex asked. And Robin had scrawled *LARRY*. It wasn't funny. It was sad. That's how it went. A few months later, I threw in the towel. Now it's just me and the remote control, the irony of whose name never escapes me.

DÉGUSTATION

--after Dante

Each time a napkin dropped they replaced it with a
new one. Folded like augurs, I couldn't drop them
fast enough. The deciduous napkins accumulated
around our feet. We were wading in a shoal of
creased linen. Our waiter was named something
like Étienne. Our waitress was Étoile. She
flickered gratuitously as she refilled our tap water.
Étienne presented grey pearls sleeping under a
sheet of pasta on a bed of oyster mushrooms. He
presented such *plats* in translation, but they could
have been anything. He said pearl and it tasted
like pearl. Although the next day, when you said
the seaweed salad tasted like semen, it didn't
work the same way. Its emerald translucence still
tasted green to me, all the more so as you then
said you didn't like it. I successfully fought back
an impulse to say something romantic about my
willingness to eat your cum. Fighting back the
impulse was beside the point since there already
existed in the air a sense that if I weren't saying
something about your cum it was only on account
of restraint. My restraint wasn't in the room but
we could maybe hear it yelping a few rooms over
or in the basement. The napkins continued to
accumulate, at this point past our knees. I reached
under the tablecloth to touch your leg, ideally
long enough to feel, from both sides, like I was
holding you, and what I thought momentarily
was your leg was the leg of our table. It wasn't
that your restraint was more coordinated than my
grabbing. You just weren't making grabs, errant
or otherwise. In a descent of further pathos, you
eventually did make a grab, but only when the
sadness caught up with the surface of my face, a
winter koi pond whose dejected and flamboyant
fish were trying their best to fake dormancy in
the dark of their pond bed, which, fascinating
for the fish, turned out to feel less frightening
than the surface to which they'd wished to think

themselves adapted. The surface, as sadness peered through, was freezing. A wind blew across it, and sadness peered through the weather, fish-eyed, incarnadine; and there was your hand on my leg, masterful and swift, like you'd done this sort of thing a thousand times, which you hadn't, not with my leg. Your hand was a nickel sending the pond askitter, the fish following, distracted, thinking girlishly along the lines of *ooh nickel*, perhaps thinking a nickel was an appropriate thing for a fish to wish on. This was all happening to my face. My hands, mercifully, were drowning in linen, which continued to rise. Only then did Étienne appear with a dish called the Meat Garden. I think I heard this correctly. Apprehensively, I tested each object and its adjacent black sauce. There, like a fig-shaped amber, was part of a pigeon, conveying its last S.O.S. And there, verily, beneath a thatch of daikon, was too large a piece of mine own heart. And with Love weeping beside me in a darkness as sudden as it was complete, I ate my fill.

ATTIC

Is where we saved special occasion china, outfits
for different seasons, paintings whose walls
we'd yet decided upon, a noose, only figuratively
speaking, a noose, the attic door clamped shut
on itself, an allegory in reverse—it closed then
opened, as this ought have been a closing, as
ought have been a different meaning. Stockpile
of dejecta and you name it, all the while mutters
to the rafters, mutters, a houseboy in adjacent ZIP
codes, adjacent streets, this whole preposterous,
in the attic. I admit my own investigation, how
few were boxes, trunks, vague memory of an
unplugged chandelier alongside bulbs that
wouldn't light for several goes. This is not our life
and is our life. There were animals in the bedroom
like there were in other, safer bedrooms, signs of
life besides the wine glasses in bathrooms, living
room, et cetera. How much witness born, who
bore this, adopted whom, as though parents could
be saved by orphans. The back door broken in
like allegory in reverse, back door broken, swarm
of pots and detritus in the sink. Little camera
of crotches, leak of tantrum under beds: the ivy
rankles as it touches, we know this now, before
we think of knowing. The bunk bed, harbor
and stockpile, lighthouse flintering its faggots, I
was there and not. I would have, were possible a
parasol conducive to blowing storms. It flurried
here, as though suspended symptom. I flurried,
cold confetti of intention. Soon we shall grill, and
plant hydrangeas, no more marjoram for seven
dollars. Traditionally, this was what onewanted
and didn't work. The attic. Strobe light lead
of leading down the attic. You watched this as
I elsewhere waited. The strobe light, what I'd
imagined, and how imagine waiting, three streets
past. I register this, brooking little and as much
as possible. And I watched, narrator in search
of character in search of plot. Little orange-belt,
sweating in downtown sun, what defense would

you perform, what block of wood your knocking.
There is more than barefoot on a plastic mat, your
feet are scorched. And the attic, if only it were
burning. Don't do this, don't do don't do, even
as I say I would, I do, but don't do this, or do, and
do, and draw the attic from its latch, muttering
stockpile, such as it is, cleared by brokedown
morning.

SOME BIG NEWS

From a slight distance, the sea looks like foil with
sailboat leftovers. The sails are down as though
the boats are grieving. I wonder if I've missed
some big news. The people in the coffee shop
didn't seem especially aggrieved. They were just
gabbing. One of them was extra-gabbing. Her son
seemed a little off. He was behind me in the coffee
line, dressed for a job interview or to spread the
word. He ordered exactly what I'd ordered. The
way he copied was strange, as though until I'd
ordered he didn't have a clue what sort of coffee
he wanted. The strangeness was confirmed when
the barista asked if he wanted anything to eat
and he stammered, as though this were the most
impossible question in the world. Maybe he was
grieving. His mom was still gabbing like a rooster,
hours past sunrise, as though sunrise was just
one moment among many. He joined his mom
at the table and buried his head in the paper. If
it had been the *Help Wanted* section, his outfit
would have made more sense. Not that anyone
dressed up in this town, not that any interview
here required the getup. He was immersed in
what seemed like an ordinary page. If it had been
a disaster, the font would have been larger so
I could read over his shoulder, this being why
disaster headlines were in larger fonts than those
of other stories, so more people know. This is
how word got round. My best guess was it was a
feel-good story about a do-gooder. Besides the
boy reminding me of Bartleby, everything was
fine. Maybe the boy would never leave the coffee
shop. Maybe the coffee shop would have to set up
across the street. Maybe the boy *was* the disaster,
cause for the lowered sails. Maybe everyone knew
the boy was the disaster but wasn't letting on;
or maybe nobody, including the boy, knew he
was the disaster. They could have been covering
something up. Nearly everyone is capable of
this, especially in such towns. I met a woman

once who lost everything in a fire, and she just
kept on playing croquet, bantering about her
child's recent graduation from Bowdoin, Belá
Fleck getting an honorary degree, how wonderful
for a banjo player to be given such a thing. We
wondered if other banjo players had ever achieved
such distinction. We couldn't think of any. She
roqueted my ball into the privet. I roqueted hers
into the ocean. We laughed and laughed against
the coral sky. No one would have guessed her
child was in the fire. Snoopers were trying to
figure out if the child had survived. Others were
mentally drafting intentionally vague condolences
that sent the right message regardless. She had,
after all, lost a lot of things. Nobody wrote, "I
wonder if your child is alive;" there was no way
of getting answers. All of a sudden I heard down
the sidewalk what sounded like Carl Orff. It was
an enormous number of kids with parents, or
teachers, or given the season, kids and their camp
counselors; or given the town, kids and their
nannies, or kids with other kids who were too old
for the swim team. Everyone, including the adults,
was holding a yellow piece of paper. Everyone was
chatterboxing. There might have been a few quiet
ones. When I was a child, I was one of the quiet
ones until I put away my childish things. But even
the quiet ones were holding yellow paper, like it
was obligatory, like a scavenger hunt. If I were on
a scavenger hunt and had to find a bunch of kids,
I found them. Maybe they were grieving. Maybe
it was another cortege and they were doing their
best to hide it. They were doing good jobs.

SWANN'S WAY (1)

That's not the way to make him active. He made
his way into a cave. He had a fine way of bringing
up his children. He would find a way of slipping
it into her hand. A way which might have led me
to believe there was an excuse. I was in no way
responsible. We mustn't go on in this stupid way.
The doctor warned her not to tire herself in that
way. In precisely the same way. Tomorrow was a
long way off. In the same way. He did everything
in the right way. I wouldn't be surprised if she lost
more time on the way. In this way they made a
critical valuation. She gossiped in this way. From
a long way off one could distinguish and identify.
Others looked best when seen in this way. I will
seek my way again. She'd never done them for us
in that way. I ran all the way to his house. Some
day I would find a way of expressing gratitude. It
volatilised itself in some way before I could touch
it. In this way, I used to sit in the heat. By way of
warning. He had a way of his own. Some special
way of life. In this way life went by. He carried me
all the way up to bed. Suspicions fell a long way
short of the appalling truth. A long way beyond
and behind it. I never knew anything more than
the way there. The way of good breeding. They
were in no way connected. I had in no way been
deceived. Anxious not to distress in any way.
And in that way distracted me from tedium. The
ways had vanished. He had been intimate in this
way. The anxious, timid way in which she begged.
The way in which she looked at him. I believe
we are going the wrong way. She doesn't care for
him in that way. The way they joke about it. The
way she told it. His way of looking at things. The
way he goes on. He recently discovered a way of
expressing it. A way of spoiling our party. Giving
way to a slight shuddering movement. In this way
I can rid myself of suspicion. I think I found a way
of getting invited. Extending a long way beyond
the province of physical desire. In the same way he

might have wiped his eyeglass. He remembered it only in a confused way. By the way, I don't know whether you're particularly well. The agony he suffered in no way resembling what he supposed. The normal way of life. In a purely mechanical way. A way of feeling intensely happy. An obsolete way of pronouncing language. Making one's way after luncheon. Still on the way to the supreme pinnacle of happiness. Way in excess of my real strength. By the way, guess whom I saw at the umbrella counter. On his way to the dentist. Divided in a different way. All the way up to the poplars.

DOUBLEBACK

Once across the border, none of the exit signs
pertained to exits. Some of the exits were closed.
Some seemed never to have existed. Some were
contemplating becoming exits, still not sure onto
what they would open. We'd stopped for photos
with the turbines. Were I with the turbines by
myself the photos would have been a cry for help.
In the long field beyond were likely bodies. We left
them in peace. We doublebacked into the big city.
It was easiest just to follow Princess, which we did
but not without another doubleback. We found
my apartment, equivocally waving its ivy like an
underwater plant. Given the state of things, and
us, we headed for a bistro. We wondered if there
was such a thing as non-wild boar. The waitress
said it would be porky, but it was more like lamb.
The waitress told other inconsequential lies, but
we were too tired to make a stink. I was too tired
for most of the boar, which ended up in doggy
bags. Up Brock Street, back on the bottom leg of
Princess, ahead of Princess turning into my alley,
we found ourselves on the fringe of the clamor
of a crazy person on a warm night in a town too
Northern to take such warmth for granted. *Who's
got a pen, I need a pen*, the clamor yelled. I had the
remnants of a boar, but not a pen. You had a pen,
and as you fished for it, the guy upped his ante: *I'll
give you a dollar*. Misinterpreting your fishing for
haggling, he re-upped. *I'll give you five dollars*. At
which point you produced a pen, which made the
guy screech into brightness. *You want five dollars
for a pen?!* We hadn't wanted money; we were just
quick studies. You said a buck was fine. Next to
our new friend, some other guy used your pen to
scribble the other's number on a scrap of paper.
This preceded by *who's got a piece of paper?* I didn't
have a pen, but I had paper scraps in my satchel.
He was trying to form the former's digits when the
former recoiled, *gimme that, gimme that, that's shit,
you can't read that*. The former grabbed the scrap

of paper from the latter and wrote in his own illegible scratch a set of digits above the scratched-out attempts of the latter. We were privy to all of this, somewhat undermining my previous insistence that nothing happens in Canada. This was happening. After the transfer of digits, our guy turned to us. *I know what you are*, he confided, in a tone so scrimmed with alcohol and maybe crack that we couldn't quite catch the tone. *I am,* I said, *but he's not. Nah,* he said. *No,* I said, *he's really not. I'm definitely, but he's not.* The exchange continued. He told us that for the sake of the pen he'd give us free dinners at *Louie's,* the restaurant at the downtown *Holiday Inn,* where, he claimed, he worked. The dinner would be his specialty, named after himself, *Fettucine Barberini,* like the faun. That he "had" a pasta was less verifiable than the *Barberini,* as he lifted his T-shirt to show us *Barberini* tattooed in a demilune above his hirsute belly. We wondered if he really worked at *Louie's.* We doublebacked home.

HATSUHANA

The boys scarce seek nor hide. Unduly bonnet-
bowing, sinewed—lash-laced, moth-wood
pinafores (as in certain cautionary tales they
crushingly are called). *Ecce* my nervy threadbare,
darting over mothwick panels innocent of
pantaloon, hermaphrodite subtext—indolence,
squalid, like there were skirmishes I'd forgotten.
Today went smoothly. We squirmed, then lobbed
rejoinders. Just sherbert mountain calligraphy,
pistachio in the horizon, as though sherbert
scoops could winnow out these cold insistent
shapes. I am a vowel upside down, the mountain
says. I might well turn over without repercussion.
We retreated to our geodes, inverted landscapes,
retreating from peacocks, laughing thrush, verso
of which is vanilla bean dropping seeds behind
the canvas. And who, returning from verso, is
this juggernaut of bliss. Dodo, we guess, and
cranes thought capable midflight of seeming
purely literary and indistinguishable from the
droppings that really prove their fluency in several
spaces. Are these birds or blots, this Darwinism
of looking painterly as whooping both from and
toward our lonely idyll. Our one and only, berries
were their wearing, inedible. And some bygone
Enoshima Strether, pondside, placid conundra
of reciprocity, the sense that romance at some
future moment might benefit from a kick in the
pants. The sherbert made us miss the Vivian
Girls—not that we needed warfare, not that so
nuts a principle could keep us from falling further
into foreground. The edges of our bargain were
fluffed, all silver rush left poofing to their own
devices. We seemed in good company, truly, so
much left unpainted, as though my folding screen
were trying to teach itself a lesson. And verily
you were saying something in a dialect of which
not even you had a firm grasp, it only being at this
point we noticed the delicate sword-bearer, stage
right, knowing, like most cupids, to arrive full-

quiver, in case he had some serious explaining. Or
was it a *koto*, a net for butterflies. *Ki-cho, sujibosi,*
halos crumbling delicately to the touch, trying
not to look too flittingly anxious about having
misplaced their respective saints. Yonder garnets
led to pomegranates like a botched trick, and
islets, amorously consumed by their own shadows,
were willing to fold into water as viciously pale
and holding as a mother not knowing what else to
do with herself. Red-handed, mouth like a sunrise,
I folded into passerine, somewhere between rare
and terribly accidental, as though a manchild
forgets lonesome, as azuline whorls right through
his more perfidious trinkets.

COTTAGES

Weekends like this, everyone has one—cookouts,
Labatt Blue, oval braided rugs from L.L. Bean,
oven mitts with scenery and cursive names of
herbs. A corner of my psyche was pretty rural but
lacked a cottage. I had an undeveloped psychical
plot, even as to desire an inner cottage seemed
a step in the right direction. Even to accept in
advance that said cottage would be a musty dump.
I didn't mind mice turds in kitchen cabinets.
I'd brush turds off tumblers with the best of
them, like residue from washing. I would learn
to love hockey sticks in mudrooms. Given that
weekends like this were for summer, I wondered
if everyone else's hockey sticks were décor. Next
to the psychical plot for my cottage was a pond,
which neither froze nor thawed. We never moved
past blueprint. Whoever was in charge had yet to
contact a contractor, intimidated by contractors,
everything. The undeveloped plot contracted
despite the weekend's humidity, whereas the other
cottages were just there, less thoughtless than
obliviously immanent, like Whitman's twenty-
eight bathers, who would have liked a cottage.
Maybe things went on there one could only
imagine. Like my landlord shluffing into some
nameless town where his stepkids perseveratingly
think about braining him on my behalf. My fridge
crisper still needed fixing. *Brain him, brain him,*
he deserves it, make some use of those hockey
sticks. *Think of him as a puck.* He's a puck. If I had
a cottage, I'd have hockey sticks in every room,
suncatchers and potholders hung from limbs
like gallows. There's a maple tree near where my
cottage should be, cracked with birds, calling to
birds across the border. Their phantom wings
flutter, trying to remember sky. And now, from
what I gather, everyone heads off to the lake,
inflatable donuts and Kawasakis in tow. Everyone
returns and listens to Canadian music. Shania
Twain has a cottage and every cottage has Shania

Twain. Let's play Stratego, missing pieces and all,
because with enough Labatt Blue, who cares. This
was where everyone was. Everyone remarks upon
newly caught fish and hockey, bare Canadian
feet padding wetly into bedrooms whose fraying
carpets smell of earlier padding feet. Better to have
a cottage, shimmying out of swim trunks, than
to wait for a landlord to fix a fridge. On Monday
they'll return, but somehow more vacant than
before, a little off, as though there were vampires
living at the end of cottage docks. They know
it. I knew it. Canoes shaped like coffins. They
can't see themselves in mirrors (which is why
Americans think they're friendly). Under other
circumstances, this could be me, escaping from
escape, already planning the return trip. I could
resume "life" "recharged," resume again. This is
where they are, parking lots of the mind, fields of
summer mind, away.

DISASTER RELIEF

If by prepared you mean Googling salmon recipes,
I am. If by prepared you mean Bloomberg speaking
in Spanish, he is. Everyone looks for safety,
scrambling from short buses like this is new. One
difference between this weekend and others is that
this one is being tracked; there are two-pronged
commas running up and down the seaboard. It's
harder to do than bunny ears. It seems to require
practice in a mirror. It's not entirely clear what I'm
trying to convey, beyond that this (two-pronged
scooping up of air, and then in some micro-disco-
like move, putting the air lower than it had been
originally) is where something might happen. The
graphic is shorthand for potential damage. The
prettiest reporters let gale-force winds play with
their hair. One reporter tosses her ponytail like
it's in a commercial; it gets across the message.
Someone should be reporting me, lemon yogurt
sauce not cutting mustard. There's no special
disaster category on *Epicurious* unless one counts
one-dish wonders. Rob Marciano regrets not
wearing the pants that go with his disaster
poncho. And here's the roof of something: we
can all relate to this. Some of the reporters got
the memo to look as serious as possible. Some
of the reporters seem to be taking the memo
too seriously. What we need is a salmon recipe
without dill. What we need is some way of not
wishing that damage be as disastrous as possible.
Tracking damage that never comes to fruition feels
like its own disaster. We can't bear the thought of
these reporters, several days later, non-ironically
referring to a tropical depression. We need some
less-ambivalent relation to being downgraded.

HUCKLEBERRY FINN

A black sail goes bust. We hitch skiffs and pull
downriver. A boy rises to surface. River rising.
Black driftwood drifting into town. Fish-belly.
Blackberries beginning to show. White sighs
from ferryboats. She's pinned. We're greenhorns.
White as snow and good for frying. Masks of
black cloth spatchcocked into fog. Way downriver
ready to jump. White and still again. Some black
thing ahead, floating. Chipped pieces showing
white, or something. Black specks on water. Were
found in rivers drowned. Aunt Sally white as a
sheet. Black clouds with rows of glowworm. A
woman in white, ready to jump. White curtains
painted with castles. Blackberries beginning to
show. Rivers, we reckon, beginning to rise. Linen
so white it hurt. I went downriver and camped for
good. Gun in hand and white hair flying. I told
him I fell into rivers. Black raft. White-caps half
a mile round. Ready to jump. Black shores for
hours. Aunt Sally white as a sheet. Rivers coming
up fast. My peeled head and white whisker. Suit
of solemn black. Dragged to door and down
to river. Sluice of white glares. Black with a
soothering way. White shirts off a line. Black as
stars and two feet deep. Fish-belly. He whitens a
little, he can't help it. Downriver under willow.
They'll hunt rivers for anything but my carcass.
The river looked miles and miles. A river like a
steamboat without lights. River and driftwood
and away. Rivers a mile wide. Go get the river
again. I tuck up river roads. Swim half across
rivers. Rivers rising. Rivers going between banks.
Relations upriver. Relations down. Ready to jump.
Drifting downriver, kind of solemn. She's pinned.
Breaking up and washing down. White as a sheet.
A boy floats to surface. I found a man in a river
setting lines. You can't tell the shape of rivers, and
you can't see distance. Black specks on water. She
churned up. I crept along and found two bodies.
They think I've been killed and floated downriver.

Then rivers softened. They were mine. Rain
in rivers looking awful pretty, always gnawing.
Edging towards the middle of rivers, nobody said
a word. When I'm downriver, I'll write a letter.
We'll have them feathered and flung. Aunt Sally
drying out. Coughing a black river. A bonnet to
match. A shovel, a river like stars. We sold him
out. We kept right along.

IT'S VOLLEYBALL, NOT SEXISM

Regardless of where one stands in terms of
volleyball being a sport or the exploitation of
affective awkwardness (e.g. *I got it, I got it, oh
fuck*). We compensate for lack of positions in
sometimes wearing protective goggles. Where
other sports have positions, we have lines that
never completely agree on their jobs. I emerge
from the locker like Alice Adams untangling
her head from a trellis. The color of my shorts is
eclipsed by their length, which is shorter than the
others. In advance of the game, still gassy-sweaty
from the poutine van, we talk strategy like the last
lonely couple in winter's kitchen, considering,
as frost stitches up our windows, the vicissitudes
of oatmeal, simmering in a cup's worth of water.
Is it okay that we used tap, should we try the
wooden spoon. Should we try it again, is it all too
late. Let's spike it. Let's assemble in formation, a
marching band without instruments—like tubas
and xylophones might drop at any moment into
our clammy hands. Our hands (our non-sexist,
needful hands) find themselves roped in what
surely is not hygienic to the extent that others
have done this, with the same sweaty net, before
us. I have the focus of Plotinus. The nudity
of my limbs is devoted to this art of swatting,
apologizing, perfunctory fist pumps. What would
it mean to win when outcomes depend, like
manna in reverse, on what doesn't hit the waxy
ground. I will die here. If marching bands were
armies, then we were marching. By which I mean I
marched, the asphalt more slippery than it looked,
requiring further precaution. I walked, carefully,
past the scrimmage of undergraduates in St.
Patrick's Day glitz. I was going home. This was my
court. I was ready, and these sad Canadian clouds
were my team. I did my best.

GOOD HONEST GUY

I find that the most desirable trait in a partner is
their immense desire for me. I'd like to think I'm
open-minded and versatile. I'd like to find "the
one" but I'm trying to get to know people before
jumping back into a relationship. I'm a scuba
diver. I'm willing to learn how to develop the bond
of human emotional intimacy with guys who are
willing, honest, communicative, and thoughtful
like me. I guess you could say that I am just a
regular T-shirt and jeans kinda guy that happens
to like guys. I am pretty much an open book so
just ask, I guess. I can be very random in action
and interest. Being a hardcore INTJ, I'm probably
at home eating candy. Each and every day, I learn
more and more about myself. I love dance music!
There I said it! I am good at researching fun
things to do. I really know what I'm looking for,
I've known since I was 20. I don't know if I have
a favorite anything. I have been called a gypsy by
nature. I love hotwings. I believe in fluid living;
this flows into everything possible. Right now I
work in the insurance industry. I'm learning to
speak Farsi. Maybe this is untrue but some things
are best left to a conversation. I have three dogs, a
gecko, and a hedgehog, so being an animal lover is
kind of a must. I have been to the other side of the
world and back which really changed my outlook
on things. I focus quite a bit on what goes on in
my body. I'd like to say I'm good at French horn
but some days are better than others. Absorbing
information is one of my joys. I've been told I'm
good at being bitchy, though you can decide for
yourself. This conversation would go smoother
if we were having it over a cup of coffee. I tend to
go towards either side of the spectrum. Cars are
amazing things to me. I want to take in as much
as possible and have a good balance of downtime
as well. Country cooking is my favorite. I am a
hopeless romantic, have a great sense of humor,
and work out 3-4 times per week. I am not looking

for HOOKUPS that is not who I am so I am
sorry if you are just looking for SEX please don't
message me. I work on a help desk and I've been
told that even though the people can't see me on
the phone that they can hear my smile in my voice.
More of my friends have cried around me than
anyone I know. I'd like to get to know you, and
figure out if there's something worth pursuing.
Let's start off with what I am and what I am not. I
enjoy being an active person. I have worked really
hard to get to where I am today. I'm self-employed,
I guess. I guess you could say I'm a big kid at heart.
Inspired creation seems to be the only thing that
matters. I love sports and the gym, but there's so
much more to me than that. I am a teddy bear who
loves to be held. I greatly appreciate at least basic
consideration for others. I could eat Mexican food
every day and usually do. I used to think I was a
city person, but now I'm not so sure. I would say
I'm a chill guy. I'm not "obviously gay," although
I know all the lyrics to *My Fair Lady*. I love puns,
and if you smell nice, that's definitely a perk! I'm
an all or nothing personality. I'm an active guy
looking to meet like-minded individuals. I am
not nearly as nihilistic as I pretend. I enjoy being
outdoors. I am a work in progress, and could
use a little help. We all have drama, but some
things could be nipped in the bud before they
explode. I don't know what it is, but people have
this tendency to end up scared that I'm going to
engulf them and devour them whole. No matter
what I write, I'm sure I can only provide a glimpse
of what I might offer. It'd be great if biking was
your preferred mode of transportation. I think
my coworkers think I'm bizarre. I like interesting
things. I've been called a Norman Rockwell
painting come to life multiple times. If you want
to know anything else, just ask. Please do not
waste my time. I seem to be really good at knowing
what I want and doing what I have to do to get

it. Overall, I'd have to say I'm a pretty good guy.
I recently purchased a fixer-upper. I probably
spend 20 dollars a month on dryer sheets. Once I
started a fire in my grandmother's house; to this
day, I have no idea how it happened. I'm usually
very busy, but I make time to free-form dance. I
am well-mannered, well-traveled, brutally honest,
earnest, and compassionate, not to mention
passionate about everyone and everything. I am
masculine and very outgoing. I can gift-wrap like
nobody's business. Sometimes, when I'm cooking,
I talk to a camera like I'm on the Food Network.
I used to write that I consider myself an average
guy, but now I realize I'm anything but. I'm one
of the good guys. You might say I could be ready
for a change. I don't want to be alone. Actively
seeking an outgoing and adventurous guy to see
where things go from here. As a teenager, I fucked
my beanbag. I'm an old-fashioned gentleman. I've
never been to Maine, but know I would love it.

SWANN'S WAY (2)

It always happened when I woke like this. Always
providing the maid with a fresh problem. Always
happy to find an excuse for another turn in the
garden. Having always had a craze for antiques. I
have always told you he had plenty of taste. That
frail kiss he always left on my lips. That line of
yours which always comforts me. That hateful
staircase, up which I always passed. Having grown
accustomed to seeing him always in the same
stage of adolescence. Always at the same evening
hour. It was always to a steeple that one returned.
Its roof always surmounted by the cooing of a
dove. Always bringing that summer back to mind.
Always preceded by a zone of evaporation. The
sensation of being always surrounded by our soul.
I've always said that he was not in the least like
other people. Always the exact opposite. Always
putting himself in their place. The unlucky
coincidence that always brought both visitors
to his door at the same time. People are always
coming to me about it. They always prove fatal.
We always returned from our walks. One always
had the wind for companion. I would always be
just on the point of asking his name. Always in
the same helpless state. Habits, which they always
imagine themselves to be on the point of shaking
off. Always a long way ahead of us, like birds.
Whom he always treats exactly as he pleases. I
am always free, and I always will be free if you
want me. There's always some excuse. His desires
always ran counter to his aesthetic taste. Having
always hitherto had the certainty of finding it.
Always until then a grotesque disparity existed.
He would always go. Since he was always tipsy.
Always finding himself dull. Always hovering.
Always trying to run with the hare and hunt with
the hounds. He would always have until then.
Always mistaking it for water. Always making a
point of letting people see that he simply must
not indulge in any display of emotion. Always

struggling to be positive and precise. Always in
that trembling condition. He always returned safe
and sound. I had always imagined it. I always kept
within reach. Why are you always talking about
that street? He has always had an insane desire
to get to know people. He must always be forcing
himself upon strangers. Always creating awkward
situations. Who always seems afraid. Who is
always free.

ROCKWELL IN BRAZIL

For the time being, shrubs were content being
shrubs. Like inside jokes or secret handshakes,
they shrubbed along in ways only shrubs
could understand. We hung our knickers on
spoonwoods near the swimming hole, scared off
butterflies, attracted melanogasters, swam our
lithe little nudities into green water, observed the
whites of our feet squished in mud. Meanwhile,
someone's absconded with our knickers. Thanks
spoonwoods, thanks for your vigilance, argus-
eyed for azaleas, pileated woodpeckers, *but not
for knickers*. We give the spoonwoods a talking
to. We ask not-so-difficult questions. Our
nudities, naired, considered each other like crab
apples blushing from neighboring branches. In
certain cultures, blushing is a form of ripening.
In others, it's like growing. We considered our
respective blushes, our mudwhite feet. We
wanted to trust each other. As you would say,
I was trying. There were serpents in the lurks,
blooming in compensation for missing bloomers.
We couldn't tell how much was going on but we
were tempted. People can, so to speak, become
anything, incomplete as they are. In this new
situation, prelapsarian, post-mudsquish, we
considered our options. Somewhere a printer was
clogging. Printers wept ink like squids mourning
virginity. Or were they tears of joy. Regardless,
they fudged our names. Of a sudden we found
ourselves surrounded by bureaucracy and dust,
like the printer was our problem, like we knew
what printers were. The file cabinets and the
clerks inside them responded to our *gosh* with
the gaze of llamas. Where'd the azaleas go? Being
naked in some foreign, saturating tedium was
as fun as it sounds. We missed Stockbridge. We
played hand games, told knock-knock jokes,
recited Longfellow, all the things that might prove
our profound innocence. Not even the dust was
convinced. No one was having none of it. How

to get into your pants if you weren't wearing
any is a real question. We played it as it laid.
Maybe the spoonwoods were in on it. Madame
Roland wept because she had not been born a
Spartan. I sympathized. Was it certain that only
soft happiness was happiness, good days being
dangerous in different ways, the lonely child
among adults drawn to Felix, the other child,
naïve to the naïve. Hey Buster, just wanted to say
hiya, let's share the casket out of which I'm falling.

THE APARTMENT
OF TRAGIC APPLIANCES

My dishwasher is a Danby Designer. It has
buttons, one of which is a blue hare pelted with
rain, suggesting the speed with which a rabbit,
seeking shelter, might clean dishes. There are
four hundred rabbits in the Aztec myth known
as the Centzon Totochtin and they are led by
Two-Rabbit, Ometochtli. Collectively they
represent inebriation, not the dregs. They wash
drunkenly, slurred between the ears. When one
pushes the blue rabbit button thinking speed, one
asks for trouble, woozling of pickle jars, peanut
butter spoons, other Danby Designer denizens
slush-piling in the alley of spinning blades. *Make
it stop spinning*, keen the Danby rabbits, *oh the
spinning*. Each morning, like a Berryman poem, I
wake the glasses up, rub off the crud like Johnny
Appleseed polishing galas on his thigh. This
rabbit, hungover from the outset, old as Aztecs:
who made this an option for a dishwasher? And
why do I keep pushing its button? This is my
Danby. It is "designer" insofar as it fits anywhere,
rolls across the scummed linoleum like it has
places to go. More specifically, I roll it from one
corner of scum to another like the desert dragging
of *McTeague*. I can only intimate how barely the
Danby washes. It heats residue only to reimagine
cleanliness as an art project. Why put things
in there at all is a rhetorical question that the
dishwasher, like one hand clapping, answers with
further questions. Then there's the microwave.
The Sears representatives were informative
if not persuasive. We expected no more from
representatives. We wished facts about reheating,
and not once did they say never expect anything
from this microwave for which already you have
paid. Not only will it not heat, it will not turn its
lazy Susan. It will warm nothing. If only laziness
were the heart of the problem. If only the problem
had a heart, roots. The laziness, like everything
else in the apartment, is a misnomer for something

serious. The microwave's own particular buttons—produce, poultry, et cetera—are pro forma. Its buttons could be pushed indefinitely (they are), and still. My lasagna is frozen. My appliances make sad food sadder, though it's rare I think about food, which is a separate problem. Separate and related, feeding off each other to compensate for things not being eaten, fed, cleaned, warmed, stored. I refuse to feel sad for the Danby or the microwave when there's so much sadness elsewhere. Like the fridge, which was abandoned for five months. Had it been a child it would have died, but it's a fridge, which doesn't keep it from nursing ongoing betrayal and resentment: *I could go on, but can't.* Oh to live in a space where all appliances are inconsolable. Who learned this from whom. There's a magnet on the fridge for a repairman, but he can only repair the surface issue. There are deeper issues in which the fridge and I commune. That something is melting. That something isn't thawing. These are pressing.

SEMIFREDDO

I'm thinking of this less in terms of gourmanderie
than a confluence of the gustative and the
diachronic, so that when you order the dessert
you don't know, temporally speaking, what
you're in for. Therefore it will need to be a French
landscape, which speaks more than most genres
to time's capriciousness. Étienne Allegrain's *The
Orangerie at the Chateau de Versailles* would serve as
a good example, the orangerie involving a flight of
stairs which surely will look different depending
on the quality of light, this being as much a
question of time as it is of color or weather, and all
this has to do with the dessert as an experiment
in inseparabilities we take for granted. And
even though the painting is of an orangerie, the
dessert is lemons, although I wouldn't rule out
the semifreddo moving toward Meyer lemons if
not mandarins, as the daylight progressed. Or
is there the possibility even of blood orange, a
delicate apocalypse. Or is *Parterre du Nord* a better
example, would this be more executable, with
its less harrowing sense of perspective. Some
versions of the semifreddo might, I suppose, be
more harrowing than others, but you wouldn't
know until it arrived, the softness of light
falling on or retreating from the most delicate
fretwork of a tree branch. The tree branches are
the darkest, least generous of chocolates, a sort
of chocolate calligraphy that itself serves as the
vehicle for what the sun is thinking, which will
depend perhaps on the amount of whipping
cream, could one play with the ratios of such a
thing, especially for the sake of replicating that
experience. There being only one way to find
out. The semifreddo being both the landscape
and the light that falls on it, as furthered by the
branch placed orthogonally across it, as furthered
by the lace cookie on which the semifreddo
rests, which might if it's not too obvious, involve
pistachio. And because temporality is as much a

seasonal predicament as a diurnal one, sometimes
perhaps the branch will sprout leaves, which of
course will not, like the branches, be imitations
of branches, they'll be real leaves. I'm thinking
at this moment of thyme sprigs (if the pun isn't
too desperate) pressed delicately into the edges of
the branch, gentle indentation of the semifreddo
itself. Or then there's something more along the
lines of aggressively misused ingredients in non-
aggressive ways. I think I've gotten here, thinking
about the tree leaves, but now it's much more
about the things one could do with cauliflower.
So much remains to be done with cauliflower,
which raises a different version of the question of
ratio. A head of cauliflower is not the same as the
floret of a cauliflower, which for the sake of our
discussion we might likewise call *chou-fleur*, if only
to illuminate the ways in which *fleur* and flower
are and are not the same, the ways this cooking
already was about not only time, but translation.
Forgiveness is an act of translation, Wimsatt and
Beardsley don't say that a poem is like a pudding,
but they do write that judging a poem is like
judging a pudding. How would one judge the use
of *chou-fleur* as purposively disorienting mode
of sprinkles. I've seen flower-shaped sprinkles,
and the oddness of the cauliflower would flicker
uncannily in and out of recognizability. Is it a very
small scoop of chocolate ice cream with sprinkles,
or is that chocolate ice cream with cauliflower
sprinkled on top of it? This is related to our
earlier discussion of the chocolate branch versus
the real sprigs of thyme—does the cauliflower
count as its own sort of sprinkle, for instance,
sprinkling, after all, being the action by which
the florets would be placed, and of course this
already is raising questions about ethics, not that
everything always goes back to queer theory, or
to paraphrase de Man, the sprinkler from the
sprinkling. So on one level this second experiment

which arises from the first involves more or less
straightforward questions of mimesis (here we're
back to French landscape), if *chou-fleur* counts
as cauliflower, if it counts as sprinkles, even
as sprinkles technically are less sprinkles than
cauliflower is cauliflower, sprinkles more or less
just being sugar. Do you see all the interesting
questions we're approaching, cascading one
after the other, how they're all related. In terms
of sugar I'd like to play with the extent to which
cauliflower, as a starch of sorts, I think it's starch,
is a sugar too, which makes it already closer to
sprinkles than we'd maybe presumed. So then the
question is how much to roast the florets, to bring
them to the point of caramelization, maybe some
of them beyond caramelizing, burnt-sugar florets,
to raise several temporal questions all at once. At
least in this moment I'm thinking the cauliflowers
would roast in maple syrup, although maybe two
separate Pyrexes, one involving maple, the other
vanilla. Or if the chocolate ice cream is sweet
enough, and the sprinkles are already so strange,
what if they're roasted with cumin, I don't think
cardamom would work, much as I wish it could.
But something about the cardamom conjures
the promising pale lucidity of a November
morning, which could be applicable to the
semifreddo. But what it comes down to is do we
use an intentionally familiar chocolate ice cream
(Breyers, even?) or is the ice cream going to need
something else, there's just so much to discuss.
Preposterous with stakes is a way of describing
vulnerability, the pathos of the semifreddo,
whether it is cold or just half-cold, and what
would that even mean, to be half-cold and sweet,
the two of us strolling in an orange garden.

SELF-HELP

I went back and forth about baggage. I could
fill it, empty it, claim it as carry-on, pay to have
it checked, but shedding wasn't something I
could do with real bags, which made the exercise
befuddling. As far as the exercise, checking
baggage seemed positive only if an airline lost it.
My bags would call no attention to themselves
beyond a wish to be overlooked in transit from
carousel to trolley to hold and back; if they
returned, they'd be snagged by someone else. I'd
make sure of it. Although losing luggage is less
common than the anxiety of lost luggage, it was
a little freeing to find myself desiring losing bags.
There would be no anxiety about the losing,
anxiety being part of the baggage. In my head, I
knew the chance of lost baggage was more likely
if the itinerary involved lots of layovers. Not that
I wanted to go anywhere. What needed to go was
the bags. And then, maybe I'd feel less sad and
self-berating and plan a trip. The baggage, actually,
didn't need to go anywhere, it needed to be lost
en route. I realized that even if my bags were lost,
they might eventually return, and the only thing
worse than having the baggage at all was the
reprieve of losing it and then its being retrieved
and left at my door. That would be the worst
day of my life. I'd open the front door humming
Hall and Oates, not even aware of my contagious
smile, and there it would be, stuffed with what I
most dreaded and to which I was most attached.
Working myself into a new panic, it came to me
that I could write on the baggage tags a name and
address other than my own. Insofar as I'd been
told on several occasions that depression was
rage turned inward, I thought I'd write the name
and address of an ex-boyfriend. While I liked the
idea of my baggage getting sent to someone who
contributed to it, it only then dawned on me,
self-beratingly, that I could leave off the baggage
tags altogether. I berated myself for having spent

so much time thinking about the tags at all.
Stupid stupid stupid! I thought going for a walk
might calm me down, but the idea of leaving the
apartment struck me as unlikely. I wondered
if walking around the apartment would count
as going for a walk, but the thought of walking
through those messy, empty rooms made me
anxious. Either particular objects inspired dread,
or reminded me of related past events. I looked
out the window. A goldfinch flew away as soon as
he saw me. I summoned the courage to boil water
for tea. I thought tea would have a calming effect.
Midway, I gave up on the tea idea and turned off
the burner. I burnt my hand just thinking about it.

BLANCHE

Old man-trap was the end of the line. As far as
farce I'd heard funnier, which didn't keep the
crowd from stitches. They whooped and crowed,
did my fellow Americans, regulation-size hands
slapping postbellum blistercloth and blondine
until the palms went claret. It brought them to me,
neither laughing nor spiriting anything, drovishly,
neither card nor cabin. Meanwhile, my lathy non-
regulation-size palm was busy with a bullet in
the brain. Where are strategically placed mirrors
when you need them, eyes in back of heads, pith
helmets. Brain, mutational, telling a body to
keep growing past folly and lintel-stoop, sweet
confused, brain, inadvertently eloquent. Pink
of persuasion, we cannot consecrate, we cannot
hallow: meet this, try to figure each other out.
What part of Red Sea don't you get, going further
biblical by the second and limsy, sorry blanched.
What's black and white and red all over? What
forrerd hyst, the keeling over, final tour of a great
nation. Never in my life have I made so many
people cry. Never so useless in assuaging. Nary
an airkiss as the train reels, nary clutch of living
fingers, catching sunset after gently mewling
sunset. I was spinning out of control, differently,
some related, likewise degenerative mutation. I
didn't end a war, I was one, or remembered having
been one, amounting to the same thing. Soon
when we survive this night, this theatre nightmare
redux, we'll tape timelines to posterboard tea-
bagged to look old, put our heads together. Was
born in a county named Hardin now called LaRue,
how rue can swallow nearly anything, calling
all outlying territory into its glassy fold. How
afterward to understand this bergamasque of
itineraries, compass needle arthritic and tired of
turning. Until then, this was the date and *I was
this*. The image of myself on stage didn't seem, as
far as mirrors go, more coordinated; it reflected
flailing with ruthless precision, unquietly. Bullet-

brained, lodged and whizzing, ardent ricochet, I
sat and watched the baroque and speedy entropy
of what, after the fact, we separately imagined as
the reflection of reflection. Reflection of curtains
rising onto smudging, warped glass of a travelling
carnival. We talked about this in a manner of
speaking. Bitters, veto, slip ticket, slingflip. I
nancied my way in and out of chairs, forgot many
things which you did not. Arrack, pupelo, dram
after dram. I wasn't pining for something lost, I
wasn't unaware that my sense of ethics required
a certain blur of fantasy and the world as such.
I really put the licks in, this wasn't nothing to
nobody, we caught a weasel sleeping. I didn't
remember being part of the problem, why one
travels with everything, negligee after negligee,
litany of negligences alchemizing into pinxters.
This is the prairillon of my discontent, populated
by animals that nose each other's noses in what
only looks like kissing. When was I recognized,
were there recounts, did you bellow, no, but boy
did I. Bullet-brain, buttonbush, all drammed out.
What is the penance for this. I could kill you, was
extreme; I could leave you, more so. I'm not quite
demolished, not yet. It's just that script, *old man-
trap*, the line that gets me every time.

SPECIMEN DAY

Every day feels like today in Bangkok. A little
hazy. Somehow someone has heaped the pallets
in advance. Softwood skids of tamarind, cabbage,
jackfruit, none of which seems to have an
opinion on anything. Various tubers in soggy
crates likewise seem not to care one way or the
other, they all look so disaffected. Or maybe
placid, maybe the gourds just know their days are
numbered, and in this knowledge have learned
a more peaceful relation to dread, as though the
gourds, leaning into each other like quiet bodies
in a bathhouse, were counting breaths, naked,
non-salacious, exhaling into Bangkok's sailcloth
sky. The sky, likewise, is more placid than usual,
so much so that it seems unaware of the ways in
which placidity itself nearly always forebodes
something or other. Pym could tell this to the
gourds, *Tekeli-li.* But the gourds, the beans, the
little eggplants are not nonplussed. Kosum and
Buppha consider their pallet of litotes. Malee
and Bussaba crack their necks, their knuckles,
all the other joints that humidity is confusing.
Kosum, Buppha, Malee, and Bussaba all mean
"flower." Flowers considering their own produce,
like affect thinking about emotion. It's nice to
think there are so many names for "flower," like
Inuits and all their words for "snow." *Tlamo,*
"snow that falls in large wet flakes." *Hiryla,* "snow
in beards." *Jatla,* "snow between your fingers
or toes." *Naklin* and *klin,* "forgotten snow" and
"remembered snow," respectively. "I remember
snow," this is a good distinction. I'd like to know
the ways in which these Thai women's names
signal different modes of flowers. "Wilted flower,"
"wrist corsage," "flower just peeking out of its
calyx," "plastic flower on a dinner table set for
one." "Plastic flower in need of dusting." They
consider their produce. Pensri considers the sky,
which is necessary insofar as Pensri means "beauty
and goodness of the moon." She watches for the

moon, waits for it, as though once the sun sets
through that thick white sky, things will really
start happening. Things are going kind of slow.
The produce, the women, equally mindful, some
of them holding parasols, one of them tonguing
something stuck between her teeth. But then,
because this is how it is every day, there are calls
of *yohk, raawk*. Of a sudden there's a need to hoist
the tarps and awnings that shadow the gourds.
Hoist, hoist, ye flowers, hoist ye fighterkite. And
hoist ye placidly, mindful of breath, how the
ropes crotchet up the pulley, the old technology
of wheels doing something we underestimate.
"Hoisting," a good word, a good name for
someone. And so tarps are hoisted. All along,
between the skids, are tracks, so narrow one might
think them flagstone paths, winding through
some amorous garden. Imagine, in the "beauty
and goodness of the moon," such a flagstone path
awakening as from a dream to this yellow train.
Good morning! This is mindfulness of a different
order. From the front, the train's windows look
like eyes and a nose, its face weaving around
the corners of dilapidated buildings. That's
how graceful the train is. It's not a bad train. It's
just a train, the way the gourds are gourds. The
hoisted canopies look incredulous, who wouldn't
be, fluttering in the train's approach, as though
the train were a breeze. It's not a "breeze," there
are several words for breeze but "train" is not
one of them. All of the dread that everyone and
everything is mindfully inhabiting gets displaced
onto the awnings. Good for the gourds to be
so ready for the next life. And nothing goes as
planned. The train is a caboose in search of what
preceded it, a caboose without expression, less
going off its tracks than proceeding upon them
impeccably. I'm mindful of the tracks, of the skids
over which the train glides without touching
anything, like Jesus. And nothing is damaged, the

women unhoisting their awnings, and it's back
to the day, the parasol, the white sky. The safety
is unbearable. Perfect train, perfect market, all
as planned. This is when you know you've met
your maker, when you know this will happen, like
clockwork, each day thereafter.

RABBIT

Klonopin, Cymbalta glow low in dusks of
bracken. Tomaselli garden with real pills in it bled
out shrubs. This is where I see him, years later.
I thump the others quiet, *put out your cigarettes*,
dimbright, *stop clinking bracelets, stop chomping,
he's here*. He was as he'd been a little older. Twigs
in his hair, like he were becoming scarecrow, or
scarecrow slowly becoming human. And there
was I in a variation of earlier birdlike outfits, fewer
patterns, more knowingly angular, theatre of
jarring neutrals. My ears twitched silver. We didn't
have words. I was real, far as that goes, though
this recent development disrupted what hitherto
had been an easy arrangement. *What's he looking
at*, I thought, *is that aura cowlicking my head again,
or were there crows*. Vision pretty much stayed
asymptotic, each squint approaching the other's
axis like a pastoral spaghetti western. The trees
were paste, the pills falling. We were ripening in
reverse, wishing we could stick everything back
as we'd found it. And so I scampered off with the
others just before the warrens vanished. Single
gleaming shape broken back into gloaming, its
being evening didn't matter, nor March nor May.
Branches, leaves. And sepals closing where just
before there had bloomed a fairy, flower-faced,
unblooming from bract like a jewel box ballerina.
She spun rusty, wand uncreaking against her
dewdrop gown. She seemed to speak in reverse.
The dizziness receded, dewdrops drying. The
pebbles of my neck still smarted from where her
wand had cracked. And there were shadows in
the velvet grass. I was leaning against a fowlhouse,
which at least bore the sound of logic. In the din
of clucks I barely noticed molecules exchanging
valentines. Blood was feathering, paling. The
further horror of the event of returning to the toy
version of oneself being that one can't respond.
I wasn't dying, I was receding, growing softer.
There was no memory of fever, there being no

memory. And I was unchucked from the heap
of dejecta, saved from fire, returned to a shelf,
the bow around my neck fluorescent with a new
vigor. The threads fraying from paws found ways
back in, homecoming of glassy parasites. I was
ravishing again and loved and barely felt it in the
batting. Soul-swaddle doesn't know the trouble
it gets into. Doesn't know all goes dark. Nor how
long in stocking. Nor scent of oranges, almond.
Placid sprig unknowing held in soft unfeeling
arms. Nor boy approaching, *stop.*

THE HOUSE OF MIRTH

Cousins inhabiting dingy houses. Visits to
relations whose housekeeping we criticized.
Where she installed herself in a house, looking
at life through screens. A woman who presumed
to have amusing house parties. The only person
who kept us in good humor when there were
bores in the house. When the house had been
too uproarious overnight. Two or three red
farmhouses dozing under apple trees. Gasping
for air in a little black house. The house being
empty. As if she had been lamenting the collapse
of a house party. The entire house deluged with
suds. It was insufferable to have such creatures
about the house. The drama of household
renovation. The house in its state of unnatural
immaculateness and order. A doorbell sounding
through an empty house. Talk of buying the
newly-finished house of the victims. Violating
the cardinal laws of housekeeping. As if there
were a contagious illness in the house. Household
expenses weighing. He reentered the house and
made his way through deserted rooms. You can't
tell what you're smoking in one of these new
houses. Annexed to her small crowded house.
Can't see why Judy keeps the house wrapped up
in this awful slippery stuff. He led her through
the house to a large room at the back. God you
go to men's houses fast. A voice warned she must
leave the house. She had once picked up, in a
house where she was staying, a translation of the
Eumenides. As the mud and sleet of a winter night
enclose a hot-house filled with flowers. If their
house was shabby, it was kept. Rattling round in
that empty house. The house was closed—Judy
telephoned this evening. We were sure she
thought her house a copy of the *Trianon*. The
house loomed obscure and uninhabited. The
housedoor closed. Something doing before she
left the house. The privilege of living in a house
that belonged to her. Striking rapidly across the

lawn toward our unfinished house. I gave up
my apartment and shrank to the obscurity of a
boarding house. A house where I could come and
go unremarked. Hating the noises of the house.
Small aggravations of the boarding house world.
Uncongenial promiscuities of the boarding house.
Once out of the house, I couldn't decide where
to go. It was strange to find myself passing his
house on such an errand. I crossed the street and
entered the house. Since it was my fate to live
in a boarding house. An image of the old house
stored with memories. The intense silence of the
house reminding me of the hour. I felt as though
the house, the street, the world were tempting.
Conceptions of a house not built with hands.
Thus adjured, I turned my eyes on the spectacle
which afforded them such legitimate mirth.

GONE WITH THE WIND

He lost it when her neck break. Grabs his gun
and shoot that pony down but he rather shoots
himself. Gets called murdersome for teaching
baby how to jump. Baby knew jumpspoon all
along, at least some picture in that pearlbrain of
hers how the jumping felt. She wrong, jump and
idea of jump colliding, as is the way. Spoiled as
pastry, cute enough for slaughter, all deathwish
coiled with a sense of irrevocable. In the manner
of Hippolytus, Phaedrus, Phaeton, pony is
unfortunate extension of ambivalent wishes
for attention, as shellgame stopgap to familial
bicker. You want cruel, you want bray, make
yourself at home. Make it. She the offspring, she
the kingdom for some comity and canard. Just
try. They be beautiful, self-excoriating and mean,
not innocent even from first punchbowl banister.
Could dressage defer barbs, dressage she would.
She and pony pony up. You can hear them in
advance, silverleafing, ponydown. Nary a mare
whiskered in pony's ear, headshy and ringsour.
Pony, phony figure of spoony dotage, knows
better and less, feels breakneck staccato down to
reticula. No stopping this pretty spectacle made
more so in our thinking we smart enough to know
how it ends in advance. No stopping boozehands
clasped around an ever-paling head. He done lost
it. He grab gun. Locks himself in a nursery with
the dead babe. And that for some time where
he stay. You both thinks you the baby, you both
thinks he's horse. We take turns with guns in
conjugal flicker. Put it down, and play as lay. And
the neck, long since broke, more persuasive than
the baby, patient past wishing until it wouldn't.
Spoony spinning ringsour without understanding
implication. Quondam spoony doesn't change
so much as reify the games, reifying what we'd
all long fretted. Look after him but never let
him know. We being everyone and everything
at once, our options shrinking to the size of a

room. Before which we watched from a verandah in whose Georgian light we convalesce from previous disasters, so many ways of falling, stairs, horse, a white ladder that would pass inspection none, but we can't live without it. Maybe some other incident will befall us, maybe we lacerate ourself with regret. Maybe he grab his gun and this time mean it. This is Mammie speaking, who earns the right to speak. Who has been emptied and filled by too many persons not her own. You gone empty Mammie what with ideas like you can't die because you already dead. None you dead, you so sorry live Mammie hurts for your living. You lie with the dead as though this was the same. And Mammie like my fridge gone lose it. She leak tears on kitchen linoleum, which don't clean tiles so much as further stain. We gots tears next to boxwine, corn chowder, snits of cheddar. Tears leave gray less gray, furthering oyster like pearls for swine. You makes Mammie all broke up. And Mammie cries for years, black hunker in a kitchen full baroque with need. This goes on like all things else needing fixing. They chips away at frozen, but still she cry tiles, as all you pace round like the fridge was the problem and not some final, incurable end. The fridge looks like a coffin, and you both in different ways thinks the other's corpsy, for whom tomorrow is another day for more reasons than Mammie can reckon. And if you kick her hard enough it might do the trick. And he still pony, he still thinking jump, heart racing like bullets in a brain. And we still whirling, we pooling together.

MILDRED PIERCE (PIE WAGON)

Nail to spackle, blueprint of houses before going
bust. Some different we builds a house from
different plans, marquetry and sliding walls. Soon
we'll have lines of Dickinson on the walls to
explain what light in any given moment is up to.
The quarry and the bait is in love, bait's vertebrae
treble-cleffing to her mirror. How she's turned out,
edges crimped like a brittle pie where hands had
touched it. As a dancer, you watch her foot as out
of nowhere it goes en pointe. Toe touches floor
like it holds a world only nearly immune to the
chaos it organizes in absentia. The ankle tenses,
ever so, the calf, I notice too, as though love made
perspicacity possible (it doesn't). Theory three.
Coloratura down to her bones, the tone in her
voice, something Mildred never heard except
in dreams. The toe just touching, reward of
training, year after year—discipline of foot barely
gracing floorboards, barely gracing. Hands try to
rest but won't, versus hands try to rest but can't.
Cantata of lassitude, sighing down to feet barely
recognizable as such, so weary-shod. Plodding
fish trucks, fancy ice cream, radio repair, Mildred
walks like a mare into pasture. Her feet hurt.
Contra Veda, whose foot, turned out, holds its
one glass note past shiver. Mildred's house can't
take care of this. No cooker, no retinue of help
make sense of Glendale, the house, the kitchen
from which all things bleed. When Mildred
apologizes for startling you, she wears her allegory,
chinoiserie, oystered up to throat. The frog is her
preference, reminder of whose voice and when,
and what it all is for. Whereas we prince frogs
less for the story than *this frog will do just fine.* Sing,
but not for me, *ribbit,* mares straggling to fields
past Laguna. Foot on pedal, showing how sound
was understood. Meanwhile not just banisters
but doors were iron, and being iron, wrought.
Let's undo garters, let's think ravened not so bad.
There were gentler forms of ravening, contra

Veda's voice presiding over books, snapdragon.
Her hands tried to hold a cigarette. The gesture
failed in all the ways Mildred fails. Block and
cleaver, all punching away at dough, away from
crimping, what turns out. We made a foot that
could walk one way or another, but for the time
being, the foot is extension of the spine. When
Veda sleeps, it is sleep of the drowned, and when
Mildred leans in to kiss that death, it is Judas in
a mirror. Pie wagon, this pertains to us only in
eating it up. To live through each other being
Lamia's song, whereas from the get-go we lived
beside. Pie wagon, endless number holding the
answer to circles, rings. Theory three, chasing
rainbow with our sharp, imagined hands. I never
kept books. I kept you happy as I could, wherein
lay the problem. Those hands had no relation
to gravity, as mine floated like moths, caught
implication. The hands went down. Throw, love,
pies in my face. These hands at ready, such as they
are, toe touching, not sure if this meant holding
or renouncing the end of the world. The house
was a ghost in advance of our settling. Everyone's
wheezing banshee, but when she puked her soul
onto the piano, when we were asked to think
of consequence, I held your dancer's foot, hand
cupping your toes, as though to say the world, it
held.

FLAHOOLEY

For some time, I'd felt flat. Less collapsed or two-
dimensional than something yeasty that had risen
as much as it could. I rose, I tried, you just couldn't
tell. Injera has a slightly spongy texture, which
means it absorbs—but only so much, only slightly,
after which whatever it was absorbing just leaks
out. That's how I felt: like the national dish of a
country famous for starving, a country plagued
with drought, which meant my sponge-like
properties only reminded everyone of something
that wasn't there. Thinking about injera when
one is starving is a particular kind of thought.
The closest some of us got to wishing I was more
around, wondering when I'd return. After great
pain a formal feeling came, and after the formal
feeling came something that felt like Yma Sumac.
Something that only a few people had heard of.
The few who had heard of Yma Sumac were split
between wanting to believe she was an Incan
princess and thinking she was from Brooklyn,
spelling her actual name, Amy Camus, backward,
like liking, for once, what one saw in a mirror,
like playing an album in the wrong direction.
This was how I felt, as though in becoming what
one had liked in the mirror, one would from that
point on avoid mirrors, because now the mirrors
reflected what one had fled. If Yma Sumac were a
Greenpoint housewife, she held this secret to her
heart. This doesn't mean there weren't moments
when Yma perhaps thought about Greenpoint,
shin-splinting down Pequod in drizzle and an
orange headscarf. Eventually, she was maybe
resigned to the fact that whatever she said likely
wasn't true, and she was as disappointed by this
resignation as she was committed to her stories.
She felt like Martin Guerre, and this was a formal
feeling. We'd put her most ambitious album to
date on the Bose, an album titled *Miracles*, so
ambitious that she was abandoned by her fans, all
of them, because they heard in *Miracles* the sounds

of hell, the fever dream of an Incan princess
making her lysergic way down the belly of a
volcano. Where they heard the sounds of hell, she
heard the chirpings of forest creatures clutching
berries, butterflies accompanying a virgin as
she swished her way to the god of the sun. As
alarming as the music itself, we grew accustomed
to it. Lynn made up interpretative dances, an eerie
macaronic of Maya Deren and past crazes like
The Frug. Jeff, fresh back from shucking corn,
not only didn't mind the music, he kind of liked
it. Jeff and Lynn thought it might be a contender
for Stuart's annual album of the summer. I was
nonplussed by how non-nonplussed we were.
At some point, Yma Sumac forgot about the
chandelier on her head, the bolts of gossamer.
When her phone rang in the middle of the night,
she answered in that infamous five-octave voice.
She used no fewer octaves when she talked to
herself, when the phone stopped ringing. Even
at her bleariest, nothing mattered more than this
gift, her craft. She worked that gift like nobody's
business. She went on a world tour that lasted ten
years, stomping off the stage in Hamburg after the
audience started laughing. Before *Miracles*, she
was on Broadway in a musical called *Flahooley*. So
a saint, when ripe for heaven, is weaned from the
world. This is how it felt.

Michael D. Snediker is the author of *Queer Optimism: Lyric Personhood and Other Felicitous Persuasions* (U. Minnesota Press) and *Contingent Figure: Aesthetic Duress from Nathaniel Hawthorne to Eve Kosofsky Sedgwick* (advance contract, U. Minnesota Press). He is also the author of two poetry chapbooks, *Nervous Pastoral* (dove|tail books) and *Bourdon* (White Rabbit Press).

Made in the USA
Lexington, KY
07 March 2014